Artistic
F*iTNESS

Artistic
FiTNESS

By Ed Tadem
Designed by Shelley Baugh
Project Editor: Meghan O'Dell
Copyeditor: Elizabeth T. Gilbert

www.walterfoster.com

3 5 7 9 10 8 6 4 2

✱ Table of Contents

✳ What's this book about, anyway?

You've probably already determined that this isn't a *physical* fitness book (we hope you've figured that out by now!). Indeed, this book is full of exercises, but these exercises are meant to tone up your drawing skills, not your (possibly) scrawny arms. (Actually, if you draw enough, you might end up with toned arms as well!)

Although we think physical fitness is important, we think it's equally important to exercise your mind and artistic talent. You may think you can't draw a straight line, but we know you can. All you need is a little motivation (check!), this book (check!), and some cheap materials (turn the page to scope them out; you may already have some of them at home).

This book will show you that anyone can draw (even you!), and that with a little practice and some dedication, you can achieve your fitness goals. Artistic fitness, that is!

✳ Tools & Materials

Pencils Drawing pencils are designated by hardness and softness. H pencils are hard and make a lighter mark, whereas B pencils are soft and make darker, black marks. I use a lead holder, which is similar to a mechanical pencil but holds only one lead at a time. I find this convenient because I can just switch out different leads and keep using the same pencil. Of course, you can also use good old-fashioned wooden pencils. I always use a rubber grip pad to minimize the strain on my hand and wrists.

▼ Sharpeners Mechanical leads can't be sharpened with regular sharpeners; you have to use a special sharpener, which you can find at art and craft stores (shown below). For regular pencils, you can use a hand-held sharpener or a sandpaper block.

▼ Erasers I use a kneaded eraser for most erasing—it can be shaped and molded to fit into small areas. And it doesn't leave those annoying eraser crumbs! Stick erasers are also great for getting into small areas. For heavier erasing, I use a regular white plastic eraser.

▼ Artist's Tape This tape is specially made to be sticky enough to hold your paper in place but not so sticky as to leave residue behind. It's also very easy to peel off without damaging the paper.

▲ **Workspace** I work on an angled drafting table, which keeps me from hunching over when I draw. I tape my drawing paper to the table with any references and preliminary sketches taped off to the side. I have an adjustable lamp on the left side because I'm right-handed; this ensures that the shadow cast by my hand will never obscure the area I'm drawing on. It's important to have a comfortable chair with plenty of back support. I also have a rolling cabinet where I keep paper and other supplies. I spread out my tools on top of the cabinet, too.

◀ **Paper** There are as many kinds of paper out there as there are leaves on trees, and each kind of paper provides different results. Bristol paper, which comes in pads or sheets, is a great choice for finished drawings. It's available in smooth (sometimes called "plate") or vellum (slightly textured) finishes. Whichever paper you choose, make sure it's acid-free to avoid yellowing!

9

✳ Warming Up

Just as you warm up before working out at the gym, you should relax your hand and get comfortable holding the pencil before exercising your creativity. I usually warm up by drawing random squiggles and lines. Familiarize yourself with the different types of lines your pencils can create, and experiment with every kind of stroke you can think of, using both a sharp point and a blunt point. Practice the strokes below and on the next page to help you loosen up.

Drawing with a Sharp Point First draw a series of parallel lines. Try them vertically; then angle them. Make some of them curved, trying both short and long strokes. Then try some wavy lines at an angle and some with short, vertical strokes. Try making a spiral and then grouping short, curved lines together. Then practice varying the weight of the line as you draw.

Drawing with a Blunt Point Now try the same lines with a blunt point. Even if you use the same hand positions and strokes, the results will be different when you switch pencils. In the example above, you can see that the blunt pencil produced different images. You can create a blunt point by rubbing the tip of the pencil on a sandpaper block or on a rough piece of paper.

▶ Starting Simply

First experiment with vertical, horizontal, and curved strokes. Keep the strokes close together and begin with heavy pressure. Then lighten the pressure with each stroke.

▶ Varying the Pressure

Randomly cover the area with tone, varying the pressure at different points. Continue to keep your strokes loose.

▶ Using Smaller Strokes

Make small circles for the first example. This looks like leathery animal skin. For the second example (at far right), use short, alternating strokes of heavy and light pressure to create a pattern that is similar to stone or brick.

▶ Loosening Up

Use long vertical strokes, varying the pressure for each stroke until you start to see long grass (at near right). Then use somewhat looser movements that could be used for water (at far right). First create short spiral movements with your arm (above). Then use a wavy movement, varying the pressure (below).

✳ Finding Your Style

After a while, you'll notice that your drawings will all take on a consistent look and feel. Don't worry—it's just your own unique style coming through. To jumpstart this process, try experimenting with the different types of linework shown below.

▶ Using Criss-Crossed Strokes

If you like a good deal of fine detail in your work, you'll find that crosshatching allows you a lot of control (see page 15). You can adjust the depth of your shading by changing the distance between your strokes.

▶ Sketching Circular Scribbles

If you work with round, loose strokes like these, you are probably very experimental with your art. These looping lines suggest a free-form style that is more concerned with evoking a mood than with capturing precise details.

▶ Drawing Small Dots

This technique is called "stippling"—many small dots are used to create a larger picture. Make the points different sizes to create various depths and shading effects. Stippling takes a great deal of precision and practice.

▶ Simulating Brushstrokes

You can create the illusion of brushstrokes by using short, sweeping lines. This captures the feeling of painting but allows you the same control you would get from crosshatching. These strokes are ideal for a more stylistic approach.

✳ Creating Form

Anyone can learn to draw by simply revisiting a lesson from grade school: Any subject can be broken down into variations of the three basic shapes—the circle, the square, and the triangle. Once you give form (or dimension) to the shapes, you'll have three-dimensional objects that seem to pop off the page. Try to think of the shapes on the left in the illustration below as real objects with solidity, depth, and weight. Then add a few lines to each to make them appear to have depth (see the center column). This is a basic example of using *perspective*, or the representation of objects in three-dimensional space (see page 16 for more information). Shading your objects with varying values—from black through grays to white—will give the shape form, as shown in the column at right.

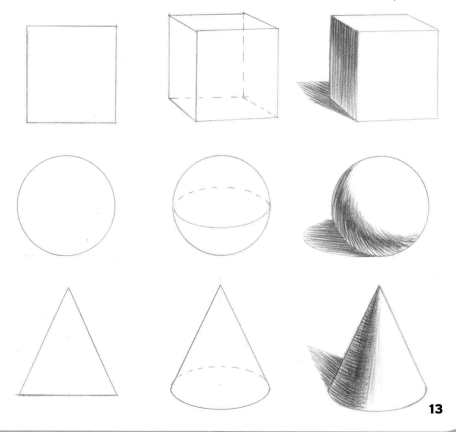

✳ Light & Shadow

Shading gives depth and form to your drawings because it creates contrasts in *value* (the relative lightness or darkness of black or a color). In pencil drawing, values range from white (the lightest value) through different shades of gray to black (the darkest value; see the value scale below). To make a two-dimensional object appear three-dimensional, pay attention to the values of the highlights and shadows. Imagine the egg below with no shading, only an outline. The egg would just be an oval. But by adding variations of value with light and shadow, the egg appears to have form. When shading a subject, you must always consider the light source, as this is what determines where your highlights and shadows will be. Keep in mind that shadows get darker as they get farther from the light source.

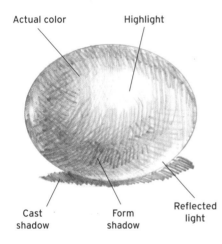

Actual color Highlight

Cast shadow Form shadow Reflected light

Identifying Values The *highlight* is the lightest value and is where the light source directly strikes the object. The gray area between the highlight and the shadow is the actual color of the egg, without any highlights or shadows. The *cast shadow* is the shadow that the egg casts onto the ground. The *form shadow* is the shadow that is on the object itself. *Reflected light* bounces up onto the object from the ground surface. (Most people don't notice that one!)

Value Scale Making your own value scale will help familiarize you with the variations in value you can produce with a pencil. The scale also serves as a guide for transitioning from lighter to darker shades. Work from light to dark, adding more and more tone for successively darker values.

✳ Basic Techniques

Below are examples of some of the most basic pencil techniques that you can use to replicate everything from smooth hair to rough wood. As you get your drawing skills into shape, you can experiment and try new techniques. Whatever techniques you use, though, remember to shade evenly. Shading in a mechanical, side-to-side direction, with each stroke ending below the last, can create unwanted bands of tone throughout the shaded area. Instead, try shading evenly, in a back-and-forth motion over the same area, varying the spot where the pencil point changes direction.

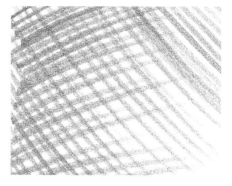

Hatching For this basic shading method, fill an area with a series of parallel strokes. The closer the strokes, the darker the tone will be.

Crosshatching For darker shading, place layers of parallel strokes on top of one another at varying angles.

Shading Darkly Apply heavy pressure to the pencil to create dark, linear areas of shading.

Gradating Apply heavy pressure with the side of your pencil, gradually lightening as you go.

15

✳ Perspective Basics

To make a two-dimensional object look realistic, follow the basic rules of perspective to make it look three-dimensional. With linear perspective, objects appear smaller as they recede (imagine a road seeming to disappear in the distance). The two most important types of linear perspective are one-point perspective (where a subject is viewed from the front) and two-point perspective (where an object is viewed from an angle). Linear perspective is important when drawing cars and buildings.

One-Point Perspective

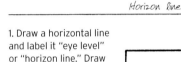

1. Draw a horizontal line and label it "eye level" or "horizon line." Draw a box below this line.

2. Now draw a light guideline from the top right corner to a spot on the horizon line. Place a dot there and label it "VP" (vanishing point). All side lines will go to the same VP.

3. Next draw a line from the other corner as shown; then draw a horizontal line to establish the back of the box.

4. Darken all the lines as shown. Voila! You have a perfect box in one-point perspective.

Two-Point Perspective

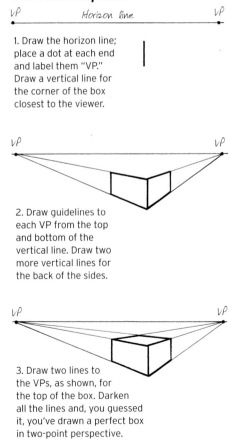

1. Draw the horizon line; place a dot at each end and label them "VP." Draw a vertical line for the corner of the box closest to the viewer.

2. Draw guidelines to each VP from the top and bottom of the vertical line. Draw two more vertical lines for the back of the sides.

3. Draw two lines to the VPs, as shown, for the top of the box. Darken all the lines and, you guessed it, you've drawn a perfect box in two-point perspective.

Foreshortening

As you learned with linear perspective, things appear smaller the farther away they become. The same is true with parts of objects. *Foreshortening* is an important method of creating the illusion of depth in a drawing, and it works hand in hand with perspective in that the part of a subject that is closest to the viewer appears larger than the parts that are farther away. To create this illusion, just shorten the lines on the sides of the object that is closest to the viewer. (In other words, make that part of the object look bigger.) Don't worry if this sounds confusing—you'll get the hang of it.

Foreshortened lines

Actual width

Side view (flat)

Front view
(foreshortened)

Chapter 1

Animals & People

✳ Penguin

Did you know that penguins don't have knees? Well, now you do. So don't draw them.

1 I start this little guy using an H pencil and basic shapes.

2 I add the wings and beak, and I start fleshing out the feet and chest. I also draw the ground.

3 I designate areas of light and shadow on the wing and head, and I start shading the body and feet with hatchmarks. Then I add the beady eye.

4 Now I shade the wings, head, and feet, following the guidelines from step 3. I also use short strokes for the fur on the chest and shade the crack in the ground.

5 I switch to a B pencil and make everything darker. Then I add a cast shadow on the ground with hatchmarks. Voilà! A penguin!

✳ Snail

No need to rush when drawing this slowpoke; remember, slow but steady wins the race!

1 I use an H pencil to draw a misshapen circle for the shell; then I add the neck, head, and tentacles.

2 I refine the basic shapes, defining the tentacles and adding the spiral pattern to the shell. I also indicate a "slime" trail.

3 I continue refining shapes and begin shading, using radial lines to suggest the texture of the shell.

4 Now I add more shading and details, such as the spots on the shell.

5 With a B pencil, I go over all my lines, deepening the shading and creating the ridged texture of the shell. And he's off! (Sort of.)

✳ Panda

Although the panda is a carnivore, its diet consists of mostly bamboo. Hence the bamboo stalk in this drawing!

1 With an H pencil, I start by drawing the rough shapes of the panda. In this sketch, I emphasize the belly of our round, fuzzy friend.

2 I construct the features, adding the ears, nose, muzzle, and leg. I also decide that the panda should be sitting in grass...

3 ...and munching on bamboo (the two things they do best!). I continue refining the features, adding the eyes, mouth, and paw. Then I create more fur and grass.

4 Now I tighten up my lines, erasing those I no longer need. I also add leaves to the bamboo and a few more details to the panda's face.

25

5 Our panda is looking too much like a regular bear, so I start shading. There we go! The black fur makes all the difference.

6 I switch to a B pencil for the final rendering, where I darken all the shading and add bamboo leaves behind the panda. Note that I fill in the black claws and pupil, leaving a highlight in the eye.

27

✳ Horse

A horse is a horse (of course, of course),
but all horse drawings are one of a kind.

〰〰〰〰〰〰〰〰〰〰〰〰〰〰〰

1 Using an H pencil, I block in a tapered rectangle for the horse's head and a cylinder for the neck.

2 Using the basic shapes as a guide, I create more defined shapes, such as the muzzle, ears, cheek, and browridge.

3 Now I add details, such as the eyes, mouth, forelock, mane, and bridle.

4 After erasing any lines I no longer need, I refine the shapes and add more details to the face and mane.

29

5 I clean up my lines even further, strengthening those I want to keep.

6 I start establishing shadow areas, filling in the pupil, nostril, and inner ears. For the mane and forelock, I use strokes that follow the direction of hair growth.

7 With a B pencil, I darken all the lines and shadows, using hatching and crosshatching to darken areas on the face and neck. I also darken under the chin and parts of the bridle.

✳ Cat

Animals don't make good live models (unless they're stuffed), so you'll want to snap a photo to use as reference when drawing them.

1 I want this cat to look like he's ready to pounce, so I make the back arched. Then I block in the head, facial guide-lines, ears, paws, and tail.

2 I round out the shapes and define the toes. Then I start using short hatch-marks to indicate fur, and I block in the eyes.

3 I continue developing the face, shading the irises and pupils and drawing the muzzle. Then I indicate the stripes on the fur.

4 I decide to start over with the eyes because they were looking too human, so I erase the shading. Then I continue to refine the lines and add more fur marks.

5 Now I establish the darks, filling in the backs of the ears and adding the whiskers. I also lightly shade the irises and make the pupil longer and more vertical.

6 With my trusty B pencil, I darken all my lines and shading. I pay special atten-tion to the eyes, whiskers, and paws in this final step.

33

✳ Seahorse

A seahorse's body looks a bit like a backwards "S." Coincidence? I think not!

❶ I use an H pencil to draw a modified "S" for the foundation of the body.

❷ Now I use simple shapes and curves to suggest the body's form. I also add the fin.

❸ I refine the shapes and add the spines on the head, the plates on the body, and the eye.

❹ I add more details to the face and further define the body plates.

5 I begin to lay down shading with hatchmarks, placing strokes closer together for darker areas. I also detail the eye and snout. I leave the ridges of the plates white to show the separation.

6 With a B pencil, I darken the lines and shading. I pull out highlights with a kneaded eraser where necessary and add a few bubbles escaping from the mouth for good measure.

✳ Cockatiel

I like drawing this kind of bird because you can adorn its head with a mohawk. And they're kinda cute, too.

1 With an H pencil, I draw the line of action, which in this case is slightly curved. Then I indicate the body and head.

2 I develop more of the bird's body, including the legs, feathers, and wing. Then I add the beak, eye, and head feathers. I also add a thin branch.

3 I continue refining shapes such as the talons, which wrap around the branch. Then I indicate feathers on the chest, wings, tail, and head.

4 Now I detail the feathers on the neck, chest, wing, and tail. I further develop the talons and face, and I make the branch thicker and curved so it looks more natural.

5 I clean up my lines and start shading the underside of the tail. I also draw swirls and knots on the branch to make it look wooden.

6 I continue to lightly shade the figure so I know where the lights and darks will be. I also fill in the pupil.

7 Now I turn to the B pencil to create the darkest areas. I strengthen all the lines, especially the outlines of the talons, branch, and cheek. I also shade between the head feathers, giving them more dimension.

✳ Dachshund

Ever wondered why wiener dogs aren't just called hot dogs? Yeah, me neither.

1 I start with a hot dog shape for the body (how fitting!), a small circle for the head, and a box for the snout. Then I draw the short legs.

2 I develop the stubby legs, draw the floppy ear and short tail, and block in the eye and nose.

3 I refine the forms and add the mouth and toes. Then I detail the eye and indicate areas of light and dark on the body.

4 After cleaning up my lines, I begin drawing fur with zigzag lines. I also detail the claws.

5 I start shading, leaving several areas of the body white to suggest reflected light. I also fill in the eye and nose.

6 Now I darken everything with a B pencil, pressing hard to make the dark areas of the coat look glossy.

41

✳ Turtle

Turtles have it so easy—whenever they don't want to be bothered, they just pull their heads back inside their shell. Wish I could do that.

1 With an H pencil, I draw a simple circle for the head and a misshapen oval for the body and shell. Then I add a line for the mouth.

2 I extend the head to form a snout, and I draw the eye. Then I add the stubby legs and refine the shell.

3 Now I create the pattern of irregular rectangles on the shell. I start making the neck look wrinkly, and I add the long claws.

4 I develop the shell pattern further and continue adding wrinkles. Turtles are a very wrinkly species.

5 Next I draw smaller shapes inside the rectangles on the shell, making the pattern more complex. Then I indicate the scales on the legs.

6 I fill in the pupil, shade the undersides of the shell and chin, and add the cast shadow. I add vertical hatchmarks to the shell to make it look ridged; I also add more wrinkles and scales.

7 With a B pencil, I darken most of my lines and shading. I add hatchmarks to the shell and skin, making it look as textured as possible. Finally, I fill in the claws and draw pebbles that hint at the dry, dusty locale.

43

✳ Guinea Pig

When drawing an animal with long fur, such as this guinea pig, use long strokes. Isn't that simple?

1 I start with a lopsided oval shape for the body. The good news is that the drawing won't get much more complicated than this!

2 Now I divide the lump into a head and torso; then I indicate the floppy ears and facial guidelines.

3 I block in the eyes and nose, develop the ears, and add the small claws. Then I start indicating the fur with long, sweeping lines.

4 Our drawing is already looking like a quinea pig, so I clean up the lines, add more fur, and draw the front claws.

5 I fill in the eyes and nose; then I start lightly shading, especially behind the ears.

6 With a B pencil, I darken all the lines and shading; I also darken the midsection to create a stripe. Now this little guy is ready to do whatever it is that quinea pigs do!

45

✳ Cocker Spaniel

These happy little dogs seem to bark incessantly, but I still love 'em.

1 I start by drawing the basic shapes of the dog with an H pencil.

2 I add the teardrop-shaped ear, the pointy tail, and the upturned muzzle. When I separate the legs, they look like baggy pants. I also draw the eye.

3 Now I start adding fur, using longer zigzag strokes than I did with the dachshund. Next I refine the small nose.

4 I continue to build up the fur, keeping in mind that this dog is rather shaggy. Then I add the mouth.

5 The mouth looks strange, so I make it look less like a smile. Then I begin shading, adding the dark spots on the ear and filling in the nose.

6 I switch to a B pencil to fill in the eye and mouth, add the whisker markings, and darken all the lines and shading.

47

✳ Female Portrait

Drawing a portrait: A good excuse to stare at a pretty girl.

1 I start this portrait by using an H pencil to draw an egg shape that I divide into thirds. Then I draw a slender neck and shoulders.

2 Using the lines as a guide, I place the ears, nose, and mouth.

3 I start to develop the nose and mouth, and I start the eyes by drawing what looks like glasses. Next I add the shape of the hair.

4 I continue to develop the features, adding the actual eyes and eyebrows. Next I add accessories like earrings, hair clips, and headphones.

5 Now I add the pupils and sculpt the nose and lips. I also draw more of the hair and add the cord of the headphones.

6 I fill in the pupils, leaving a highlight in each, and then I start shading. I leave her bangs mostly white to show that they're dyed blonde.

7 With my B pencil, I darken all the lines and shading. The headphones and back of the hair are the darkest areas.

49

✳ Male Portrait

Want to make a friend happy? Make him look like James Dean when you draw him!

1 As with the female portrait, I start with an oval and divide it into sections. Note that the guidelines are slightly curved because the head is at a three-quarter angle. Next I draw the broad neck and shoulders.

2 I use the guidelines to place the eyes, nose, and mouth. Then I add the ears (the one on the right is barely visible) and the jacket.

3 I start refining the features, adding the eyebrows and lips. Then I draw the shape of the hair. I also draw the collar of the T-shirt and develop more of the jacket.

4 I continue to develop the features and add details, cleaning up my lines as I go.

5 Now I fill in the pupils and block out the light and dark areas on the figure. This fella is starting to come to life!

6 Using step 5 as a guide, I begin shading, adding details like the ribbing on the shirt collar and the seams of the lapel. Then I draw some scruffy stubble on his chin.

7 I switch to a B pencil and darken all my lines and shading, especially under the jaw and on the neck.

51

Chapter 2

Fantasy Creatures

✳ Dragon

Come on, stop pretending that you didn't play Dungeons and Dragons in high school (or last night, for that matter).

1 I use an H pencil to draw a snaky body shape, which I divide into sections.

2 I develop the body, adding wings, legs, and the facial features.

3 I draw the lines on the underside of the neck and torso, as well as the spikes along the dragon's backside. I also add more details to the face.

4 I develop the drawing, strengthening the lines I want to keep and erasing the rest. Then I start shading the far wing.

5 I begin shading the rest of the body, indicating the scales and ridges. I make the front wing more detailed, which helps the far wing recede into the background. Then I fill in the eyes, add the cast shadow, and draw a rock on the ground next to the dragon.

6 As usual, I darken the lines and shadows with a B pencil. I erase the cast shadow on the neck from step 5, as it made the drawing look cluttered. Should it be there? Probably; but the drawing looks better this way.

55

✳ Mermaid

Mermaids aren't known for being very nice; they lure people to their death! But they sure are pretty.

1 A mermaid should look flowy, so I start this drawing with arcs and swoopy lines. You can already tell what some of the lines will become, like her hair and tail.

2 I start filling in the figure, finishing the tail with a crescent shape. Then I add the arms, torso, and features.

3 I develop the face, tail, and flowing hair; then I add the seashell bra and build up the arms.

4 I continue softening the forms and adding details, such as the gills around her hips.

5 I let my pencil wander around to create the hair, making it look organic and wild. Then I indicate more scales and clean up all my lines.

6 I draw bubbles around her gills and tailfin for interest. Then I thicken certain lines and start shading the few areas that need it, such as the scales and seashells.

7 With a B pencil, I complete the final shading, being careful to keep the contrast between her soft, smooth human half and her thick, textured fish half.

57

✳ Gargoyle

Despite their ghoulish appearance, most gargoyles aren't bad guys; their ugly mugs actually ward off evil spirits!

❶ I use an H pencil to sketch this crouching mythological beast, adding facial guidelines for placement.

❷ I use the guides to block in the facial features, and I rough in the forms of the body and wings. I also add a tail that hangs off a ledge.

3 I continue to flesh out the figure, making it look muscular. Then I detail the wings, hands, feet, and tail. Note the claws on the tips of the wings.

4 I develop the face, shading it to look sunken. Then I start shading the wings and body. I lengthen the top bone of the wing at right and add more sharp claws.

59

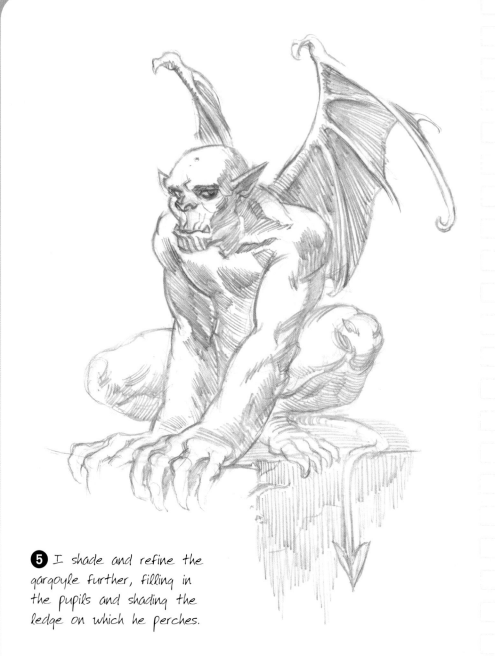

5 I shade and refine the gargoyle further, filling in the pupils and shading the ledge on which he perches.

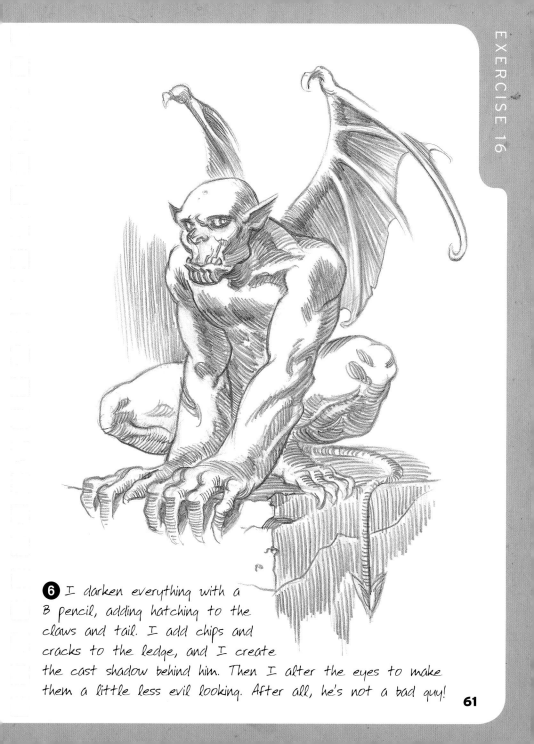

6 I darken everything with a
B pencil, adding hatching to the
claws and tail. I add chips and
cracks to the ledge, and I create
the cast shadow behind him. Then I alter the eyes to make
them a little less evil looking. After all, he's not a bad guy!

✳ Pegasus

It's a bird! It's a plane! It's...a horse with wings!

1 I start by drawing the torso and head of a horse with B pencil; then I suggest the arched legs.

2 I build up the general forms, including the legs, tail, and ears. Then I add the wings, and it's a Pegasus!

3 I continue fleshing out the forms, adding details such as the eyes, nostrils, and hooves. I make the mane and tail flowy to suggest motion.

4 Now I clean up my lines and create the individual feathers of the wings. I also add more hair to the mane.

5 I start lightly shading, mostly making sure that the far wing doesn't look like it's growing out of the Pegasus's head.

6 I switch to a B pencil so I can darken my lines to create the final rendering. I also add more shading to the underbelly to help the foreleg advance forward.

✳ Pixie

Pixies aren't always all sugar and spice and everything nice—let's draw an eerie-looking one.

1 For this little mischief maker, I use an H pencil to sketch the pose of the figure.

2 Now I construct what looks like a mannequin over the sketch. I also block in the shapes of the wings and add facial guidelines.

3 Using the facial guide-lines, I block in the eyes, nose, mouth, and ears. I refine the shapes, defining the clawlike fingers and indicating her outfit. Note that the wings look like curled leaves.

4 I decide to turn the head so it faces the viewer, so I make the necessary adjustments. Then I continue refining the forms. I also draw the hair (complete with a flower) and detail the outfit.

5 Now I clean up my lines, strengthening those I like and want to keep. I also indicate some light shading.

6 I continue shading, making the hair dark but leaving a band of white to suggest a headband. I also add leaflike veins to the wings. Then I fill in the eyes, making them seem otherworldly. I also shade the back leg to make it more distant.

68

7 Switching to a B pencil, I darken all the lines and shading. I add small hatchmarks to the wings to darken them, and I draw dark rings around the eerie eyes.

✳ Chapter 3

Food & Drink

✳ Apple

Drawing an apple a day keeps the doctor away!
(Wait, that's not it...)

1 I start this drawing by blocking in the basic shape with an H pencil.

2 I indicate the plane of the top of the apple and the pit that slopes into the stem, as well as the cast shadow.

3 Now I refine the shapes and clean up my lines. I also add quick strokes to the front of the apple for the form shadow.

4 I start to fill in the values using hatchmarks. I use curved lines on the lighter right side.

5 I continue shading, leaving a white highlight. Then I darken the stem.

6 Switching to a B pencil, I deepen the shading, making the darkest areas the left side of the apple and the cast shadow.

✳ French Fries

Fitness tip: When you crave fries, try drawing them instead of heading for the drive-through!

1 I start by using an H pencil to draw a box for the...well, the box. Then I add the general shape of the fries.

2 Using the general shape as a guide, I draw individual fries and round the edges of the box. Then I start the box's logo.

3 Now I define the fries, giving them shape and form. I make them turn in different directions so they look more natural. Then I continue refining the box and logo.

4 I clean up my lines and shade the hamburger patty on the logo. I also add a long highlight on the right side of the box to indicate the shiny material.

5 I begin shading the left side of most of the fries, being careful not to overdo it. I also shade the left side of the box and fill in the border on the logo.

6 As usual, I switch to a B pencil and darken everything. I add a few spots of tone to some of the fries to make them look more realistic. You can almost taste the salty goodness.

✳ Martini

When drawing a martini, it never hurts to add a few olives. All this drawing is making me thirsty.

1 I start this martini by using an H pencil to draw an upside-down triangle on a stick. I use ovals for the base and olive.

2 I start refining the shapes, drawing the liquid and an olive on a toothpick inside the glass.

3 I continue to clean up the lines, giving form to the liquid and suggesting the cast shadow and a little olive juice.

4 Now I apply some rough shading, leaving parts of the glass white to indicate the liquid. I also leave the insides of the olives white.

5 With a B pencil, I darken the shading and outlines. Then I drag the eraser over the glass to indicate a reflective surface. Bottoms up!

✳ Pineapple

Despite its spiky surface, this fruit is used as a symbol to welcome people in some cultures.

1 With an H pencil, I draw an oval for the pineapple and add two curved lines for the shape of the leaves. Then I draw a criss-cross pattern that curves around the form of the pineapple.

2 I draw the leaves, making them smaller and more condensed at the base and wider and longer at the top.

3 Using the lines as a guide, I create the diamond shapes. Rounding off the edges gives the shapes form and makes them appear three-dimensional.

4 Now I add spikes to each diamond shape, making sure they point upward.

5 I start shading the undersides of the leaves and spikes, as well as the spaces between each diamond shape.

6 Using a B pencil, I darken the shading, emphasizing the grooves between the shapes and darkening the left side of the pineapple.

79

✳ Coffee Cup

Nothing will wake you up in the morning like drawing a nice, hot cup of java!

1 I start by using an H pencil to draw a tapered cylinder and a basic circle overlapping the cylinder.

2 Now I define the lip of the cup, add the jacket, and detail the lid.

3 I continue to add details; then I suggest the cast shadows.

4 Now I clean up my lines, erasing any I no longer need. I also indicate the logo on the jacket and the circle on the side of the cup.

5 I begin shading, creating the liquid inside the cup and adding a steaming coffee cup to the logo. I also fill in the hole in the lid.

6 With the B pencil, I darken all the shadow areas. I leave the horizontal lines on the jacket fairly strong to suggest a ridged texture.

✳ Ice Cream Sundae

Draw me! Pretty please?
With a cherry on top?

1 I use an H pencil and basic shapes to start this drawing, which looks kind of space-agey at this stage.

2 I refine the shape of the glass, adding a fancy curved edge. Then I indicate the blob of whipped cream and the cherry.

3 I continue developing the forms, adding streams of fudge on the ice cream and wavy lines on the glass to indicate a reflective surface.

4 I add more details to the glass and start shading the fudge so I don't get confused. Note that you can see some of the fudge through the glass. I also refine the cherry stem.

5 Now I shade all over the ice cream and glass, adding tone to the cherry and filling in the rest of the fudge. I also shade the glass, leaving some areas white.

6 I use a B pencil for the final rendering, making the fudge the darkest value and softening the shading on the ice cream. To finish, I erase some areas of the glass to make it look shiny.

✳ Sake Set

Looks like I'm thirsty again. Let's draw a traditional Japanese sake set, shall we?

1 First I block in modified cylinders for the cups and bottle with an H pencil. I add a tilted cup inside another cup for interest.

2 Now I refine the shapes, erasing any unwanted lines.

3 I add a flowery design to the bottle and cups, adding cast shadows for each.

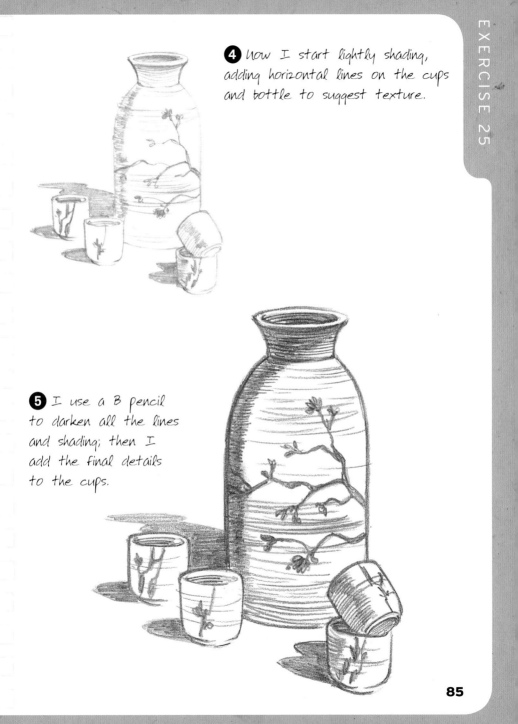

4 Now I start lightly shading, adding horizontal lines on the cups and bottle to suggest texture.

5 I use a B pencil to darken all the lines and shading; then I add the final details to the cups.

✳ Lunchbox

So it's not really a food or drink—but it contains them! Wasn't life so much easier in the days of lunchboxes?

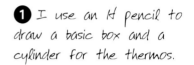

1 I use an H pencil to draw a basic box and a cylinder for the thermos.

2 I develop the shapes, rounding off the corners and defining the lids.

3 Now I add both handles and a border for the front of the lunchbox. What good is a lunchbox without a fun picture on the front?

4 I decide to go with a Hawaiian theme, so I draw a palm tree, some waves, lines for the sky, and the sun.

5 After cleaning up my lines, I start shading the sides and back of the lunchbox, as well as the lid and handle of the thermos.

6 Switching to a B pencil, I darken all the lines and shading. I keep the shading on the side of the lunchbox irregular to give it a metallic feel.

✳ Wine Still Life

This pretty much speaks for itself, don't you think?

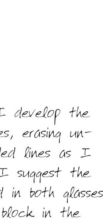

❶ To start this classic still life, I use basic shapes and an H pencil to sketch the wine bottle, glass, and cork.

❷ I develop the shapes, erasing un-needed lines as I go. I suggest the liquid in both glasses and block in the wine label.

❸ I continue developing the forms, adding some spilled wine around the cork and distorting the line of the bottle as seen through the glass.

4 Now I start shading, leaving white areas in places to suggest reflective surfaces. I also add cast shadows, a tear in the foil at the top of the bottle, and a piece of foil attached to the cork. I texture the cork with small dots.

5 I switch to a B pencil and darken all the elements, taking care to leave the highlights as white as possible.

89

✳ Sushi

Did you know that "sushi" actually refers to the rice itself, which is often topped with fish or meat? You learn something new every day.

1 I use an H pencil to draw the shape of the sushi tray, as our sushi rolls need something to rest on. Then I add two lines for the chopsticks.

2 I add thickness to the plate and chopsticks; then I draw the cylindrical rolls, using guidelines to line them up.

3 Next I sketch the garnishes: ginger, wasabi, and a decorative veggie. I also erase the guidelines.

4 I start developing the details, using square shapes for the fish. Spicy tuna, perhaps?

5 I start indicating the textures of the seaweed and rice, erasing guidelines as I refine the outlines. I also add shading to the inside corner of the plate.

6 Now I begin some simple shading, continuing to add texture to the elements.

7 With a B pencil, I darken everything, making the tray and seaweed the darkest. Looks good enough to eat!

91

✳ Chapter 4

Still Lifes & Other Objects

✳ Bonsai Tree

The perfect plant is a drawing of one:
No water necessary!

1 With an H pencil, I rough in the shapes of the bonsai tree and its box.

2 Now I refine the shapes, making the trunk twisted and using loose ovals for the clumps of leaves.

3 I tighten up the lines a bit and draw a little flower design on the box. I also add short strokes for the leaf texture.

4 Now I start shading, creating the foliage and the texture of the box. I also add more twisty lines to the trunk.

5 Switching to a B pencil, I darken all the shadows. Note that I leave the tops of the leaves white to indicate the light source.

✳ Retro TV

Watching TV might rot your brain, but drawing one certainly can't hurt!

~~~~~~

1 To draw this boob tube, I use an H pencil to draw a simple box in perspective; then I throw on some legs.

2 I add some rough details (screen, knobs, buttons, antennae, and the like), using a ruler to make straight lines.

3 I continue to add details and then clean up my lines with an eraser.

4 Now I start lightly shading, indicating the rounded screen and the cast shadow.

5 I use a B pencil to darken and tighten up all my lines. On the screen, I darken the lines as they get farther from the light source.

✳ Tiki Totem

Unfortunately, you probably aren't in Hawaii. But you can imagine being there by drawing this Tiki totem!

1 I use an H pencil to start this Tiki totem with a rounded cylinder; then I add some grass at the base.

2 I block in the features, making my lines angular to look wooden.

3 Now I add details and refine the forms, erasing any lines I no longer need. The curved lines suggest a carved depression.

4 I begin shading, making the eyebrows, nostrils, and lips the darkest areas. I also darken the grass and add more blades.

5 With a B pencil, I darken all my lines and continue shading, keeping the shading uneven to help create the appearance of carved wood. Finally, I add more grass.

✳ Scooter

The next best thing to owning a scooter is drawing one, right? Well, maybe not, but it's still fun.

1 I use an H pencil and basic shapes to block in the scooter.

2 Now I add the handlebars, seat, light, kickstand, and wheels.

3 I add more details and erase unneeded lines. Then I add the curb and some pebbles on the ground for interest.

4 Now I start shading, adding cast shadows for realism. I use wide cross-hatching on the floor-plate for texture.

5 Switching to a B pencil, I darken the shadows and edges, making them pop. Now this scooter is ready to ride!

✴ Retro Clock

Use a ruler to make straight lines in your drawings; admit it, you're not THAT perfect.

1 I start this clock by using an H pencil to rough in a three-dimensional, upside-down triangle with legs.

2 I begin refining the shapes, adding details and rounding out the forms.

3 Using a ruler, I divide the clock into 12 parts and add the numbers. Then I roughly sketch the pinup girl. I make the numbers on the left side only partially visible to show depth.

4 I refine the shape of the girl and carefully clean up all my guidelines.

5 Now I begin shading, filling in the girl's dress and legs and adding the clock's cast shadow. The shadow along the top of the face of the clock helps give it dimension and form.

6 With a B pencil, I darken all my lines and deepen the shading. I also add some dark spots to show metal reflections on the surface of the clock and the legs.

✴ Gnome

You've seen him in lawns everywhere, but have you ever drawn this ubiquitous gnome? Here's your chance!

1 First I rough in the round body; triangular hat; and blocky hands, feet, and lantern with an H pencil.

2 Now I refine the shapes and place the features and details.

3 I add more details to the gnome and lantern, and I indicate light and dark areas. I start shading the facial features and beard. I also draw the stone base.

4 After cleaning up my lines, I follow the guidelines from step 3 to begin shading. I leave the front of the stone base free from edges to show that light is directly hitting it.

5 I use a B pencil to tighten up all my lines and deepen the shading, creating dark grooves that give the drawing a sculpted look. Now this gnome is ready for garden duty!

105

✳ Sneakers

Here's the ideal pair of shoes: They won't hurt your feet and they'll never smell bad.

1 I use straight lines and an H pencil to block in the rough wedge shapes of these shoes.

2 I continue adding lines to indicate the major forms of the shoes, including some of the laces.

3 I draw more laces, laceholes, and the pattern on the bottom of the shoe. Then I draw a circle for the branding and indicate some folds in the fabric.

4 I finish drawing the laces and continue adding details, especially on the rubber soles.

5 After cleaning up my lines, I start shading, adding cast shadows and a dark circle on the side of the front shoe for the branding.

6 Switching to a B pencil, I darken the lines and shadows until I'm happy with my drawing.

Buddha

This statue is known as Budai, or the Laughing Buddha. Hey, I'd be laughing too if I had all those treasures!

1 I start with a rounded triangle for the general shape of this jolly guy.

2 Now I roughly sketch the major elements within and around the triangle, including the head, belly, and folded legs, as well as the arms and the objects they hold.

❸ I start to get more specific with shapes and planes. Now you can see the ears, fingers, and toes.

❹ Now I add the facial features, creating the happy expression. Then I refine the fingers and develop the shapes of the objects, such as the necklace. I also add the belly button.

5 Now I go to town with the details, refining lines and adding shapes. I also indicate the light area on his bulging stomach.

6 I lightly fill in the shadows and other dark areas, giving form and dimension to the statue.

7 With a B pencil, I really push the darks. I leave the chest and top of the belly white to show the light source. He sure looks happy, doesn't he? Guess that's why he's the Laughing Buddha!

Guitar

If you can't play the guitar, don't worry—now you can impress your friends with a drawing of a guitar.

1 I use an H pencil to draw the number 8 (or a snowman, whichever you prefer). Then I add straight lines for the fretboard (that long neck thing, for those of you who don't speak guitar).

2 I add form to the base of the guitar and block in the basic parts (the soundhole is the circle and the bridge is the rectangle). I also erase the lines in the neck.

3 I add more details, such as the strings, frets (the horizontal lines on the fretboard), machine heads (the bolts on the uppermost part), and the strap.

4 Now I start shading, mostly concentrating on the fretboard, strap, and soundhole. I add a few horizontal lines to the front of the guitar to suggest the wooden texture.

5 I use a B pencil to darken everything, emphasizing the raised frets. Notice that although I don't draw every string going up the fretboard; your eye fills them in.

✳ Maneki Neko

Draw this cat for extra luck—you're going to need it if you want to sell your art!

1 I use an H pencil to draw a sphere for the head, a bean for the body, and rounded triangles for the ears.

2 Now I refine the forms and delineate the limbs. Next I add the curved facial guideline, the oval coin hanging down from the collar, and other details.

3 Using the guideline, I block in eyes; then I draw the nose and mouth. Next I add the spots and define the toes.

4 I continue adding details, such as the triangular claws, round pupils, and lettering on the coin. Then I indicate some of the darker areas.

5 I start shading, filling in the spots, ears, and pupils. Note that I leave highlights in the pupils.

6 I darken the outline of the cat to make it look more like a statue; then I add tone to the claws, collar, and coin. I also suggest the cast shadow.

7 As usual, I darken the lines and shading with a B pencil. I use heavy pressure on the spots and pupils to make them look shiny and painted. Finally, I draw the dark whiskers. This drawing is the cat's pajamas!

✳ Dashboard Hula Doll

If you can't date her, draw her!

1 I use an H pencil to draw a stick figure with a curved spine.

2 Now I add basic shapes to fill out the form. I also suggest the arms.

3 I keep fleshing out the forms, adding her face, hair, hands, feet, skirt, and flowers.

4 I refine the eyes and mouth, and I use poofy shapes to define the flowers. I also refine the skirt.

5 I clean up my lines, darkening the ones I want to keep. I also develop the hands and feet.

6 I start shading, focusing on the hair and coconut top. I decide that she doesn't really look like a figurine, so I add a circular base under her feet, which I also shade.

7 I use a B pencil to make everything darker; I concentrate on the grass skirt and the shadow it casts on the legs, as well as the shadows on the figurine's base. I keep my shading loose in this final stage.

✳ Fedora

While the popularity of Indiana Jones's trademark hat may just be a fad, your hat drawings will never go out of style.

1 Using an H pencil, I draw the basic structure of the hat and add the line for the wide band.

2 I change the shape of the top of the hat to make it look folded in, and I draw a curved line for the "dimple" in the side.

3 I clean up the lines a bit, erasing some of the guidelines and adding the bow on the band.

4 I clean up my lines even further, giving form to the hat with curved lines to show the brim's roundness.

5 Now I start shading, changing the direction of the strokes to show the form. I leave most of the dimple white to make it look sunken in.

6 With a B pencil, I darken all the lines and shading. I go over the edge of the brim to give it more weight and thickness. Indy would be proud.

121

✳ Sign

You might think drawing a neon sign in black and white wouldn't be as fun as drawing it in color, but I beg to differ.

1 With an H pencil, I draw intersecting rectangles in perspective and the classic arrow for the sign.

2 Now I give form to the arrow and add a guideline for the neon bulbs. Then I add the lettering and the shape of a saxophone.

3 I use the guidelines on the arrow to place the neon bulbs, and I add guidelines at the tip of the arrow. Next I add the beams that support the sign.

4 I give form to the lettering, making it look like a neon tube. I also give shape to the beams and add the small lights at the tip of the arrow. Then I round off the edges of the sign and detail the saxophone.

5 After cleaning up my lines, I start shading the edges of the sign and cast shadows on the beams.

6 With a B pencil, I darken everything, especially underneath the letters and bulbs to make them pop. The ampersand and sax are painted, so they can be flat. Finally, I add shading to the front of the sign to make it look weathered.

123

✳ Mini Cooper

When drawing cars, you might want to start small. Anything named "mini" is a good start!

❶ I start by drawing a boxy shape with an H pencil. Then I add the headlights, wheels, windows, door, and grille.

❷ I add details, such as the license plate, mirror, bumper, and the reflectors on the grille. I also round out the shapes and give them form.

❸ I keep adding details, including drawing the roof and seats as they're seen through the windows.

4 I add even more details, including the hubcaps, insignia, plate number, and windshield wipers. I clean up my lines as I draw.

5 I start shading lightly inside the car. I also shade the headlights, tires, door handle, and other details.

6 Now I use a B pencil to shade more thoroughly, concentrating on the headlights, grille, underside of the car, and tires. Note the radial strokes on the tires.

125

✳ Robot Toy

We all know you still like to play with toys. At least now you can do something useful with them!

1 Using an H pencil, I block in the shape of the robot with squares and curved rectangles.

2 Now I develop the basic shapes, erasing un-needed lines.

3 I block in the eyes and nose, and I add details such as the "joints" and screws.

4 I add more details, indicating the fingers and making the feet look like they can bend.

5 I clean up my lines and add more definition, especially to the kneepads, as they were looking too flat.

6 Now I start shading, giving all the parts more form and dimension. Note that shading the top of each square in the chest makes the squares look concave.

7 With a B pencil, I darken all my lines and add shading with hatching and crosshatching. As a final touch, I make the fingers look flexible and add cast shadows under the upturned feet.

127

✳ Piggy Bank

You know what they say: Put your money where your pencil is! (They do say that, right?)

1 I start this money receptacle by drawing an oval with an H pencil.

2 I round out the oval a bit, making it a little more circular. Then I place the ears, snout, legs, and tail. I also add the facial guidelines.

3 Using the lines as a guide, I draw the eyes and nostrils. Then I clean up my lines and add the coin slot.

4 Now I darken the lines I want to keep and erase the rest.

5 I start shading, mostly on the underside of the pig and inside the ears, nostrils, and coin slot.

6 I use a B pencil to darken the lines and shading, making the edges of the pig pop.

7 Still using the B pencil, I add a bit more shading to the surface of the pig, along with some highlights to suggest a shiny surface.

✳ Record Player

Apparently, vinyl is making a comeback. When did it ever go away?

1 This portable record player starts as an open box, because that's basically what it is.

2 Now I divide the inside of the lid with guidelines. Drawing an "X" helps find the midpoint of rectangular shapes.

3 Using the lines, I place the inside label, handle, and latch. I also draw an oval for the record.

4 Now I add more details, such as the top latch, a speaker, the corner bumpers, and the needle and knobs.

5 I start to erase guidelines; then I round off the edges of the box and detail the corner bumpers.

6 I start shading, making the bumpers black. The rectangle on the side becomes a speaker simply by crosshatching for texture.

7 Switching to a B pencil, I complete the shading. The hatching on the box is some-what irregular, providing a subtle texture that seems sort of worn and antique.

✱ Orchids

Did you know that vanilla comes from plants in the orchid family? Again, you learn something new every day!

1 With an H pencil, I draw a tapered cylinder for the pot and simple lines for the main stalks of the orchids.

2 Using the stalk lines, I build up the flower shapes and add more stalks. I also add the leaves and develop the flower pot.

3 I continue developing the flowers, making them look more organic. I also work on the pot, giving it a softer, more interesting shape.

4 Now I clean up my lines and add more details. I also add texture to the pot with horizontal hatchmarks.

5 I start shading, adding texture and shadows as I go. Note that the elements no longer look flat.

6 I use a B pencil to complete the shading, including a shadow under the lip of the pot. I darken some lines and not others to separate and distinguish all the different shapes.

133

✱ Retro Chair

Furniture makes a great drawing subject because it doesn't move. Or talk.

❶ I use an H pencil to draw a stick figure of the chair. Note that I "draw through" the seat to place the chair legs.

❷ I build up the form of the chair, adding curves for a retro feel.

❸ I refine the shapes and add details, such as the edging of the chair. I also make the legs thicker.

4 I start shading a bit, making the back legs and undersides of the arms the darkest. I also shade under the seat cushion.

5 With a B pencil, I darken the lines and intensify the shading, though it remains minimal. Finally, I create the cast shadow under the chair.

135

✳ Salt & Pepper Shakers

What's better than a pair of fez-wearing monkeys? A pair of fez-wearing monkeys that also make your food taste better!

1 To draw these simian salt and pepper shakers, I start by drawing the blocky shapes of the bodies, heads, and hats.

2 Now I develop the forms of the monkeys. I keep in mind that these aren't real monkeys, so I retain the blocky shapes.

3 I define the arms, legs, and feet. Then I block in the facial features and write "S" and "P" on the hats to make it more obvious that these figures can be found in kitchens, not in the wild.

4 Now I indicate the fingers and toes, as well as the mouths. I also add dimension to the letters on the hats.

5 I clean up my lines, erasing those I don't need and darkening those I want to keep.

6 Now I use a combination of horizontal and vertical lines to start shading. I leave areas white to suggest a reflective surface. I also add the cast shadows.

7 Switching to a B pencil, I darken all the lines and shading, avoiding the highlights to suggest a shiny surface. I also add some holes to the top of the "S" hat for an extra touch.

✳ High Heels

Shopping tip: Drawing designer shoes is a heck of a lot cheaper than buying them.

1 High heels like these have a very graceful nature, so I start by drawing some elegant curved lines with an H pencil.

2 Building on my lines, I suggest the toe and the heels.

3 Now I make the heels thicker and construct the back of each shoe.

4 I continue developing the shapes, cleaning up my lines as I go. I also create the toe opening.

5 I refine the lines I want to keep and add the label to the inside of the shoe.

6 Now I start shading, mostly concentrating on the insides and undersides of the shoes.

7 I switch to a B pencil to darken my lines and shading, making sure the shoes look separate. Then I add cast shadows to make the heels look more substantial.

✳ 1940s Car

I'm sure drawing a classic car will come in handy someday...

1 I start this car by using an H pencil to draw one small rectangle on top of a larger one.

2 Now I round out the form and add details such as wheels, headlights, windows, and the bumper.

3 I continue to add details and develop the forms, erasing lines I don't need.

4 I add details to the wheels, grille, and body of the car. Then I draw the seats inside.

5 I clean up all my lines, refining and adding more details as I go.

6 Now I start shading, leaving the roof, parts of the hood, and most of the side of the car white.

7 With a B pencil, I darken the lines and shading, paying special attention to the grille and fenders. Check out the classic white-wall tires!

143

That's all, folks!

Well, that's about it for this book. Is your arm sore from all that drawing? I sure hope so! Just like any fitness program, you should repeat these exercises as often as possible. And don't get discouraged if your drawings don't look exactly like mine do. Everyone has his or her own style—if all art looked the same, it would be pretty boring! Just draw everything as often as you can, from the girl sitting across from you to a crumpled soda can on the ground to your own two feet. Soon enough, your drawing skills will be more toned than Arnold Schwarzenegger's muscles.